Dinosaur Mazes

Roger Moreau

Sterling Publishing Co., Inc.
New York

10 9 8 7 6 5 4 3 2 1

Published by Sterling Publishing Company, Inc.
387 Park Avenue South, New York, N.Y. 10016
© 2000 by Roger Moreau
Distributed in Canada by Sterling Publishing
℅ Canadian Manda Group, One Atlantic Avenue, Suite 105
Toronto, Ontario, Canada M6K 3E7
Distributed in Great Britain and Europe by Chris Lloyd
463 Ashley Road, Parkstone, Poole, Dorset, BH14 0AX, England
Distributed in Australia by Capricorn Link (Australia) Pty Ltd.
P.O. Box 6651, Baulkham Hills, Business Centre, NSW 2153, Australia
Manufactured in the United States of America

Sterling ISBN 0-8069-5929-0

Contents

A Note on the Suggested Use of This Book

As you work your way through the pages of this book, try not to mark them. This will enable you to take the journey over and over again and will give your friends a chance to take the same journey that you took with all of the same dangers that you have to face.

Special Warning: When the way looks too difficult, avoid the temptation to start at the end and work your way backwards. This technique would be a violation of the rules and could result in your inability, while in the past, to return to the present.

Cover Maze: Many of the dinosaurs in this scene are not happy with your presence. Find a clear path to the base of that distant volcano for momentary safety.

INTRODUCTION

The period of time the dinosaurs flourished upon the earth is called the Mesozoic Era. It lasted for nearly 150 million years, from about 250 to 65 million years ago. That era is broken down into three time periods: the Triassic, Jurassic, and the Cretaceous. The Triassic period was a time when there was just one great continent called Pangaea. During the Jurassic period, Pangaea had divided into two large continents called Laurasia and Gondwanaland. In the Cretaceous period, these two continents continued to divide until the continents looked almost like they do today.

Nothing can strike fear into one's mind than the thought of coming face to face with a hungry, meat-eating dinosaur. In 1841, when Sir Richard Owen gave the name "dinosaur" to the bones that were being discovered, he must have imagined that kind of fear, because the name means "terrible lizard." From those fossils, and ones that have since been found, paleontologists have been able to reconstruct what these animals looked like. Thanks to the creative abilities of the movie industry, that terror is accentuated when we see realistic-looking dinosaurs live again on the screen. Fortunately, there is never any real danger.

Even though a lot is known about how dinosaurs generally look, there are many specific characteristics that are imagined. What if someone could actually return to the Mesozaic Era and get real photographs? Think how valuable to the scientific world they would be. Now, thanks to special computer chips, it is possible to transport a willing photographer back to the age of the dinosaurs. Just put this chip into the computer and off you go! All that is needed is a volunteer.

How about you! There will be unbelievable dangers. It will take great courage. You will have to take with you a laptop computer in order to return. And don't forget your camera. Oh, and thanks for volunteering. To get under way, just turn the page.

J-Chip

When you plug this final chip into your computer terminal, you're ready to transport yourself back to Mesozoic times. Find the right path to plug in the "J" chip.

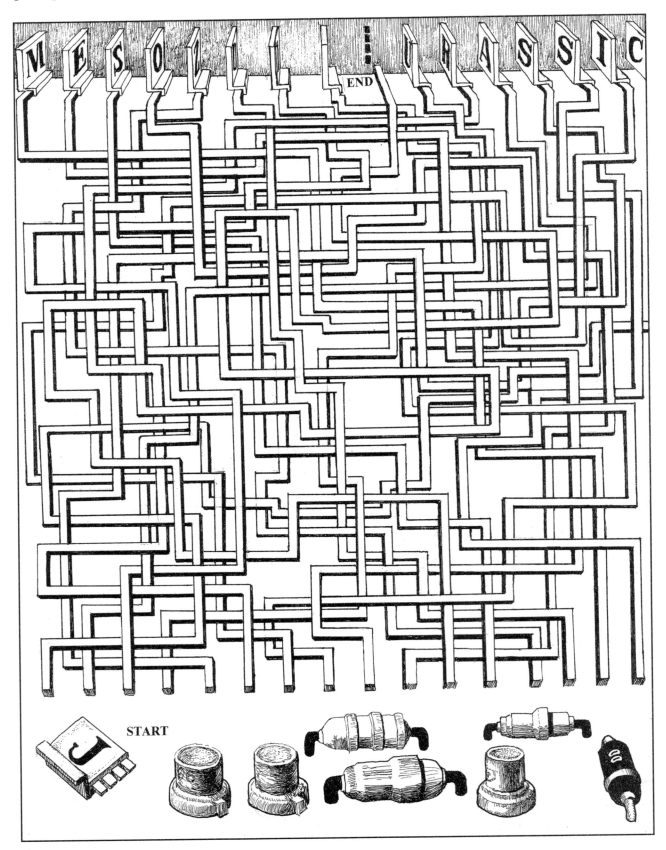

The Keyboard Setup

Put all 11 letters onto the proper letter pad by following each pathway from the letter to the pad. Then type in the period of time you want to travel to. Next, press ENTER . . . if you dare!

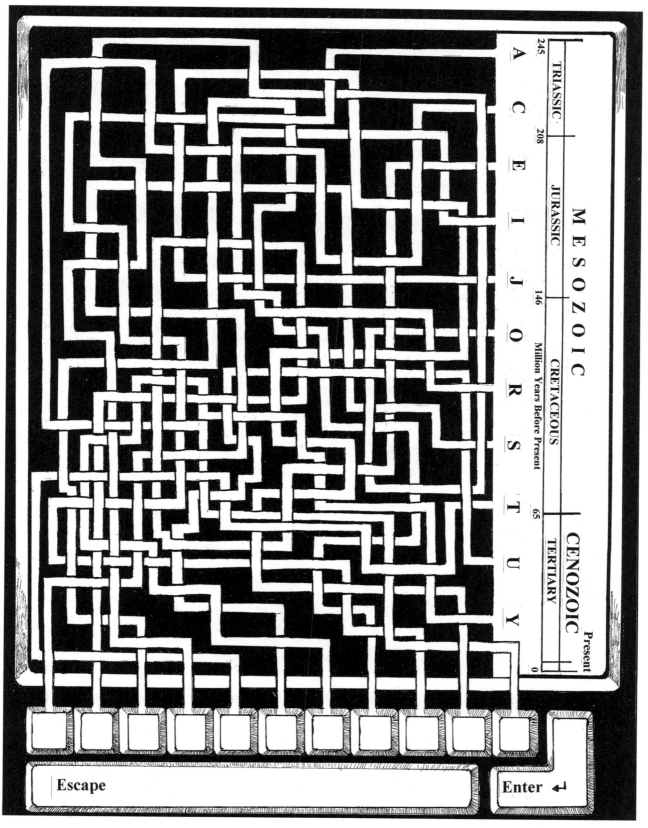

Allosaurus! Look Out!

It's obvious the transfer worked. This *Allosaurus* is looking for a meal. Set your lap-

Start here

top computer down to lighten your load. You can get it later. Keep your camera and escape from the dinosaur by avoiding the cracks.

Safety this way...

Velociraptors!

This place doesn't look any safer than the last place you were at. Those raptors

START

have their eye on you. Find your way over the canyons to the rock cave for safe-ty.

The Nest

This is a tender scene. This mother *Maiasaura* is asleep. Get a photo of each egg by

START

finding a path to each egg without backtracking or crossing over your own trail. Hurry before that dragonfly lands on mother's nose and she awakes.

Feed the Brontosaurus

This plant eater is friendly if you feed him. Find the vine that will get you to the limb, feed him some leaves, and take a close-up photo before you descend.

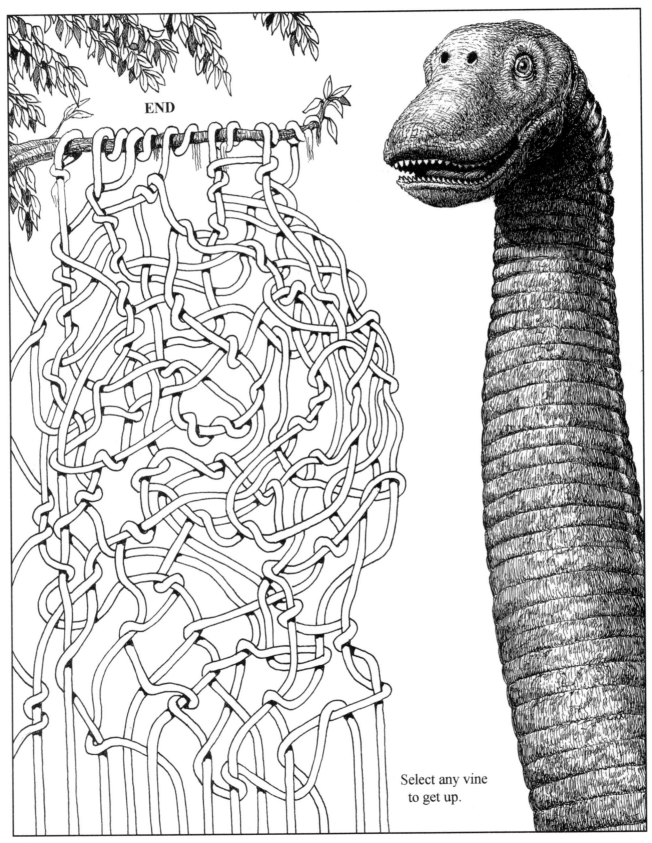

END

Select any vine to get up.

The Welcoming Committee

You'd better choose wisely when you select the vine for your descent. Each one of the raptors is hoping for a meal.

Switch to any vine to get down.

END

A Brontosaurus Herd!

Find your way around the *Brontosaurus* to the clearing on the upper right.

START

END

The Battle Is About to Begin

No time to waste here. This *Tyrannosaurus* and *Triceratops* have some real differences. Clear out fast by finding a clear path to the top of the hill.

START on any path. **END** at the top of the hill.

One Giant Foot Coming Down

This foot of a 78-ton *Brachiosaurus* is about to come down on *you*. You've got 60 seconds to find a clear path to the far side of his shadow.

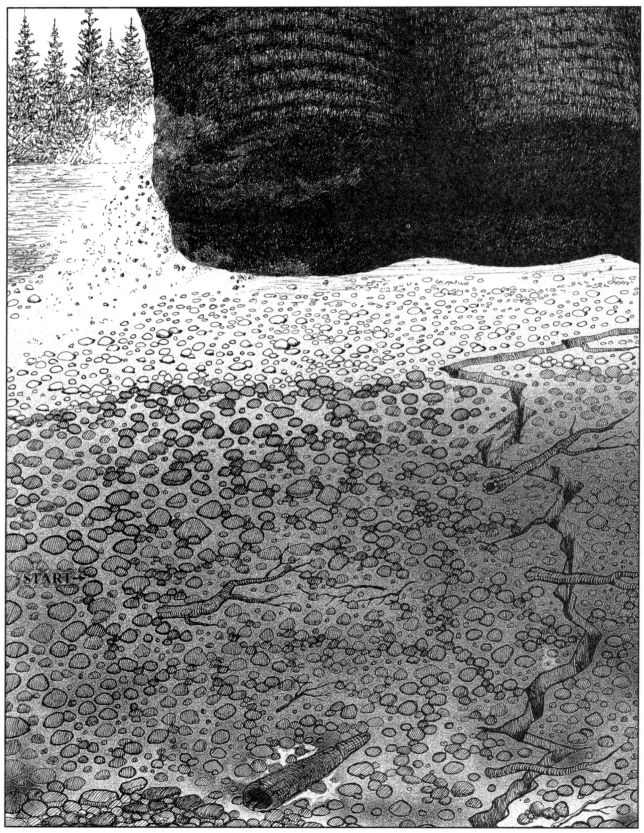

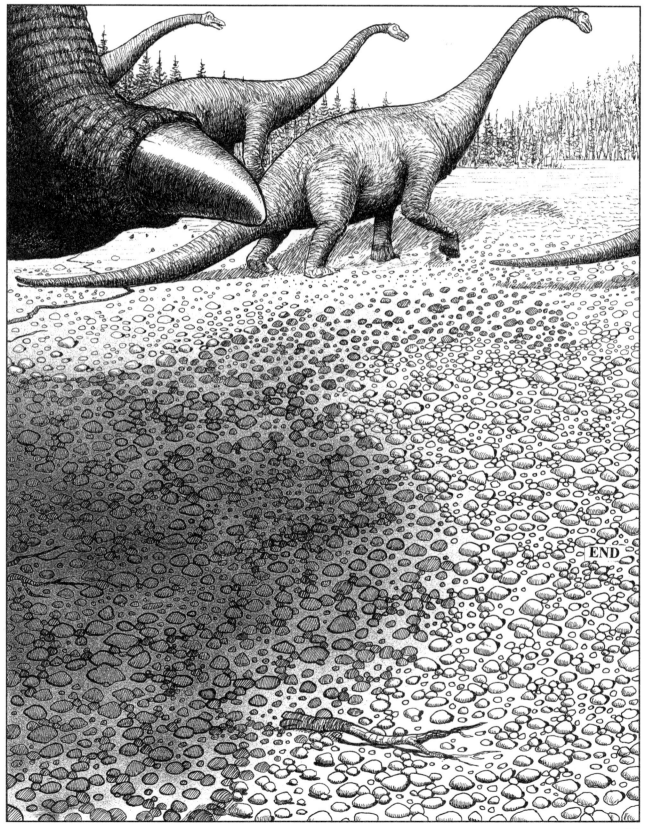

END

Head to Head

Two *Pachycephalosaurus* are butting heads to win territory, while a third one awaits

his turn. You'd better move to the top of the hill while there's still time to find a clear path.

The Tar Pit

A *Stegosaurus* is sinking into this tar pit while it's mate looks on. Move out onto the connecting logs to get a close-up photo and then exit on the right.

START

END

A Direct Hit

Euoplocephalus has made a direct hit that is bringing down this *Tyrannosaurus*. You've got 30 seconds to avoid the cracks and get out of the way.

START

ESCAPE →

An Aerial Threat

These *Rhamphorhynchus* are looking for food that crosses into a shadow. Rapidly cross this area by staying in the sunlight.

START

END

Photograph the Nest

While the adult *Pteranodon* is looking for food, climb the connecting rocks and photograph the babies. Be careful not to drop your camera.

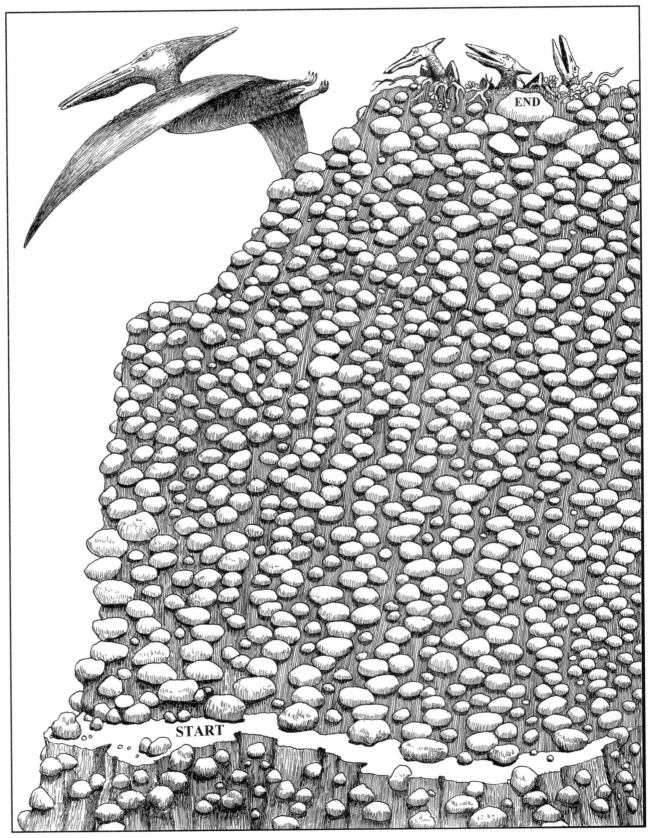

Retrieve Your Camera

Your falling camera has knocked out a nesting *Pteranodon*. Descend the connecting rocks to pick up your camera before he awakes.

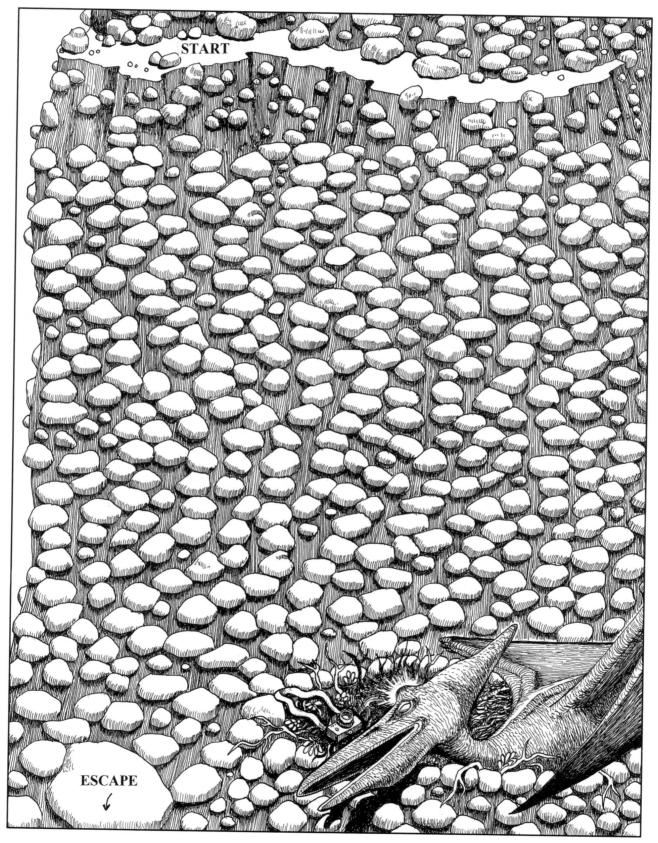

Create a Fossil Bed

This is a potential fossil bed if you can remove that fallen tree to let the mud flow

START

32

over these remains. As you make your way to the tree, don't touch any of the remains.

Earthquake

During these prehistoric times, earthquakes were common. Find your way to solid ground near the shaking tree. Avoid the cracks.

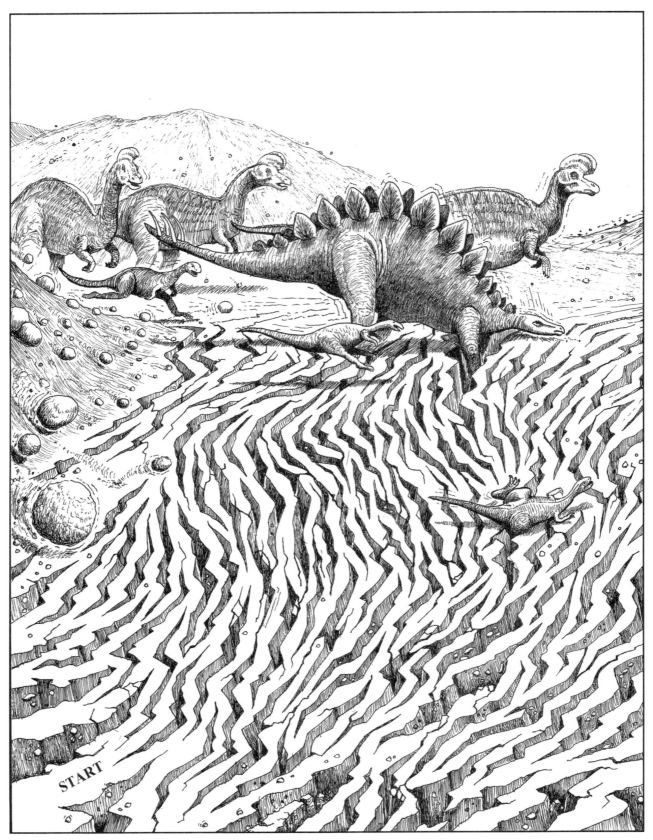

START

SAFETY HERE

Volcanic Eruption

It's raining hot rocks from that distant volcano. You have 30 seconds to find a clear path around the dinosaurs and get out of this place.

ESCAPE →

The End Is Near

A huge asteriod that will end the dinosaur era—and you—is near impact. Your

START

laptop computer is where you left it when you arrived. Avoid the dinosaurs, get to it as fast as you can, and hit ENTER. Good luck!

END

Name the Dinosaurs

You made it back! Great. From your photo album see if you can name the

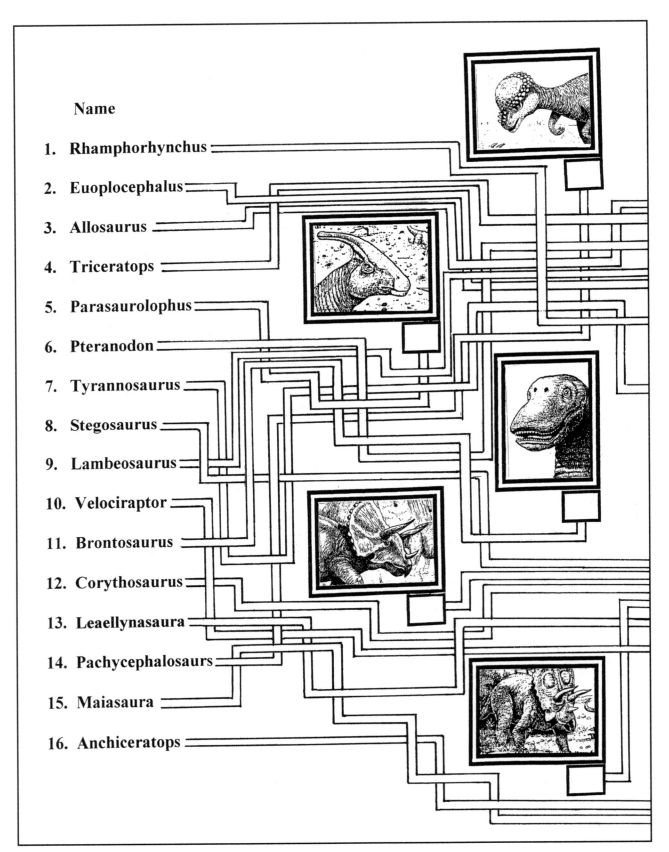

Name

1. **Rhamphorhynchus**

2. **Euoplocephalus**

3. **Allosaurus**

4. **Triceratops**

5. **Parasaurolophus**

6. **Pteranodon**

7. **Tyrannosaurus**

8. **Stegosaurus**

9. **Lambeosaurus**

10. **Velociraptor**

11. **Brontosaurus**

12. **Corythosaurus**

13. **Leaellynasaura**

14. **Pachycephalosaurs**

15. **Maiasaura**

16. **Anchiceratops**

dinosaurs without looking back. Place the number by the name under the picture of that dinosaur.

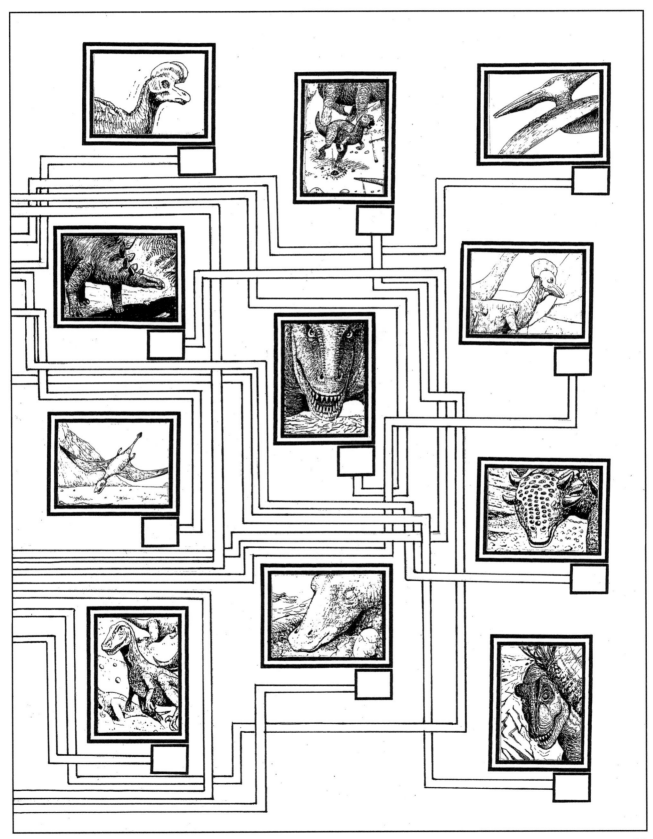

Congratulations

What you have accomplished will go down in history as equal to if not greater than any of the great explorations—including exploring the mysteries of the great oceans and walking on the moon. Your photographs will be in every publication. You will be honored by leading scientists, top universities, and world leaders.

More important, you have demonstrated great courage and a willingness not to give up even in the face of the most terrifying of circumstances. You are to be greatly admired. Now, see if you can find someone else who is willing to volunteer as you did and go back to the Mesozoic Era. The world can always use more photographs. Just crank up the computer and away they'll go.

Special Guides for the Mesozoic Era

If you had any trouble finding your way, you can refer to the guides on the following pages. It is doubtful, however, if you had trouble, that you survived. Below is a guide for the cover maze.

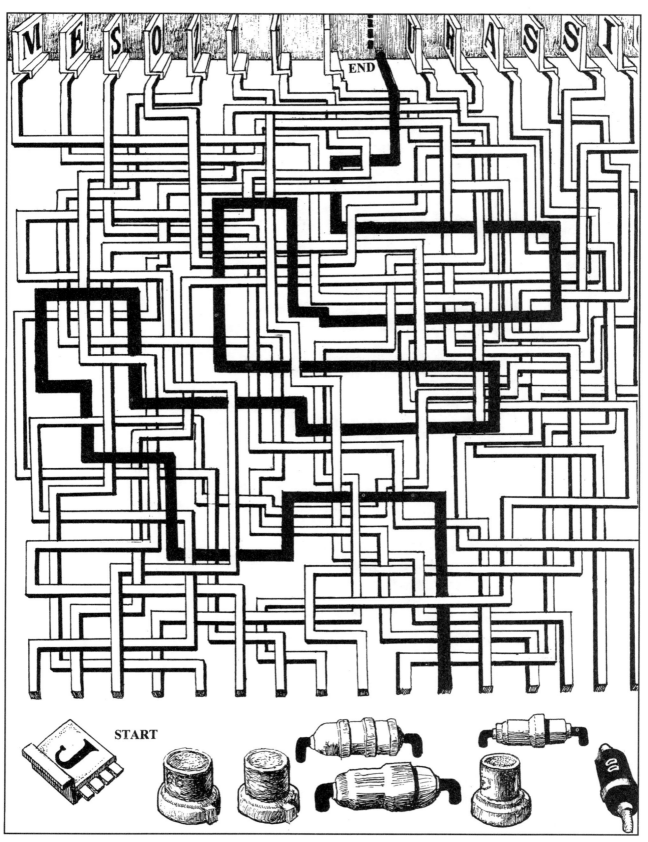

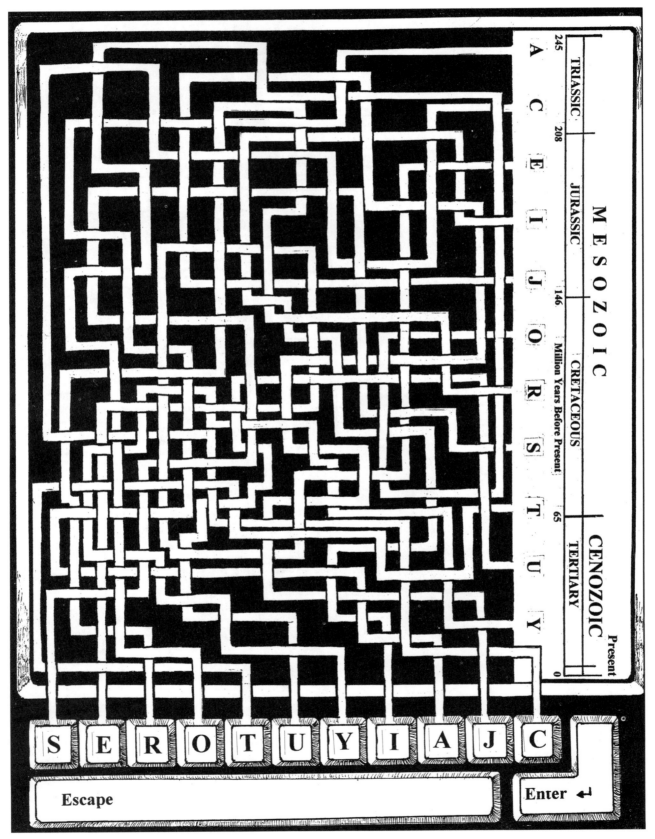

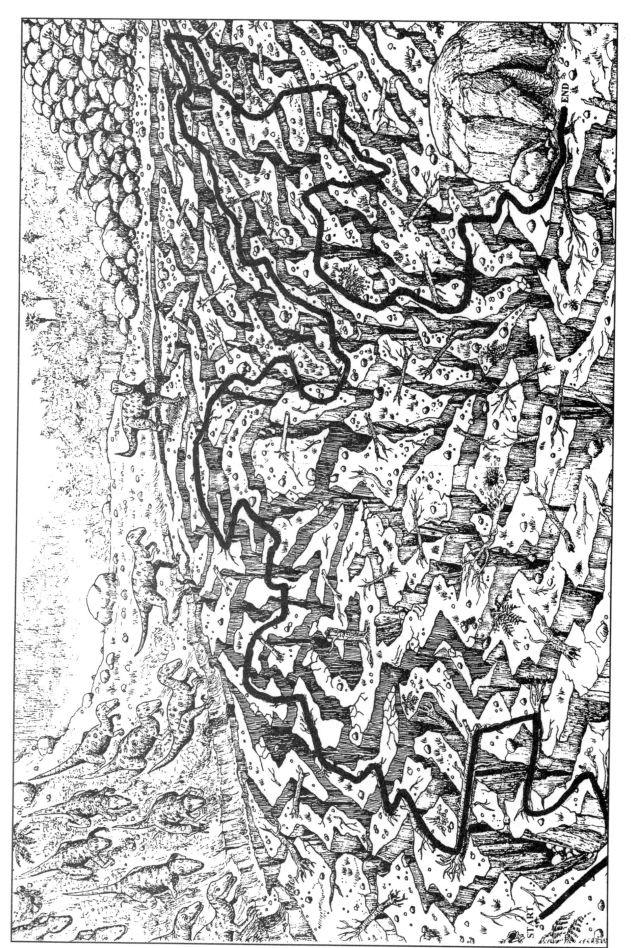

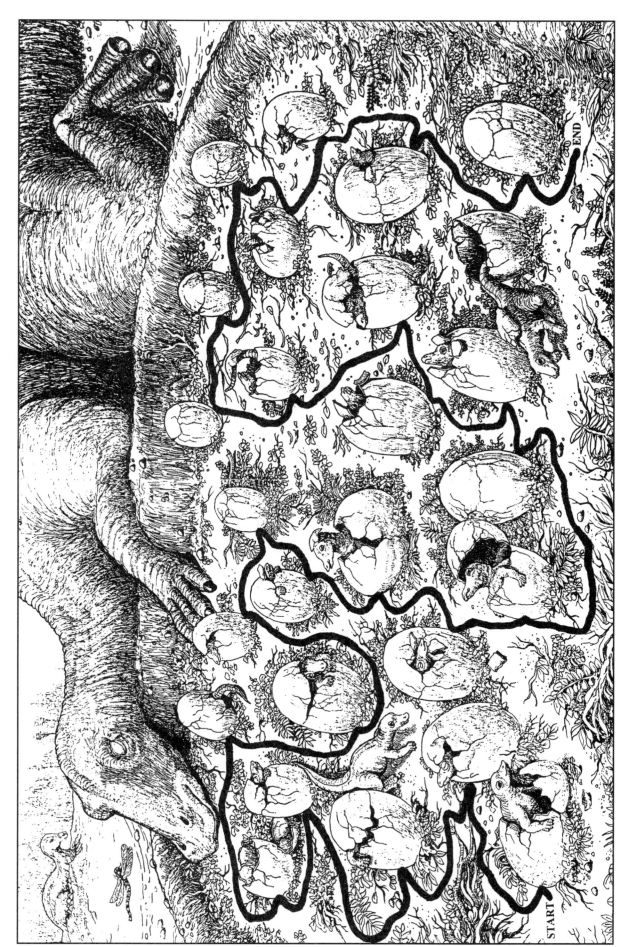

Feed the Brontosaurus

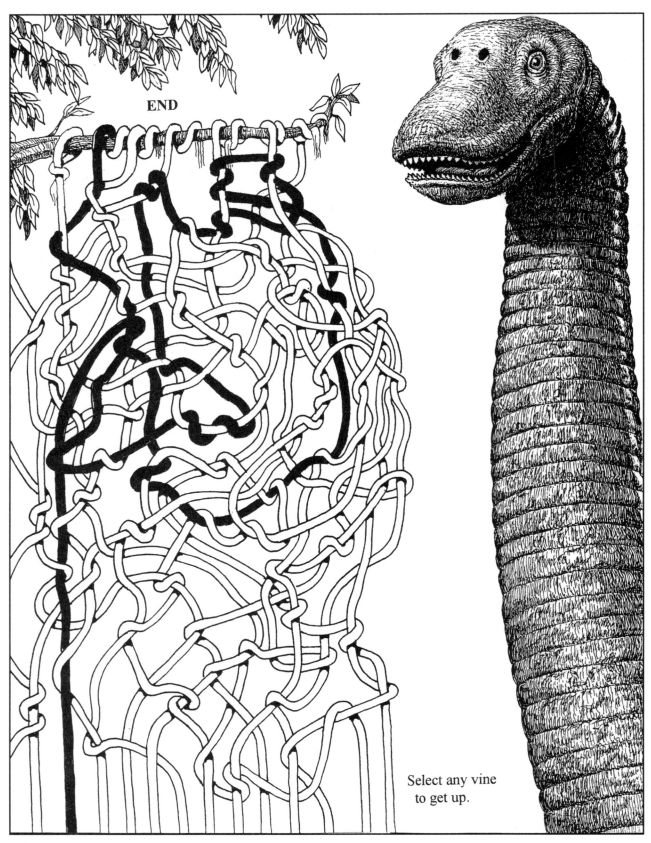

END

Select any vine
to get up.

Switch to any vine to get down.

END

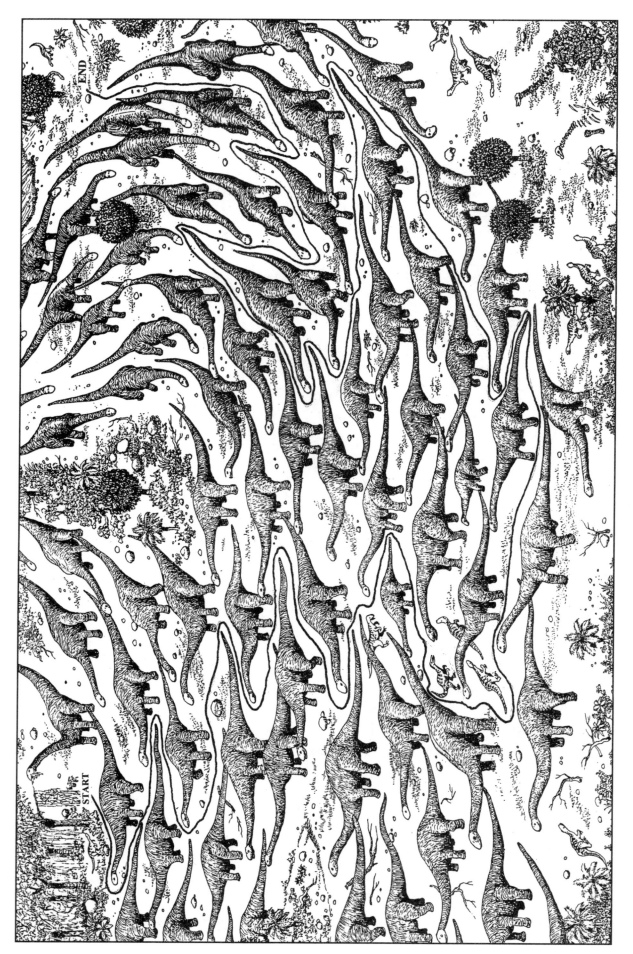

START

END

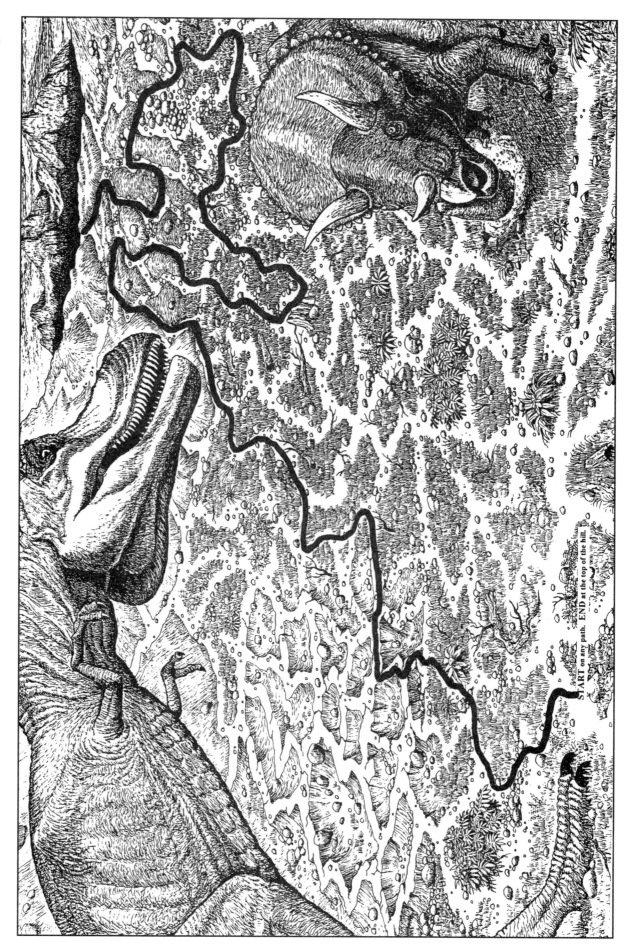

START on any path. END at the top of the hill.

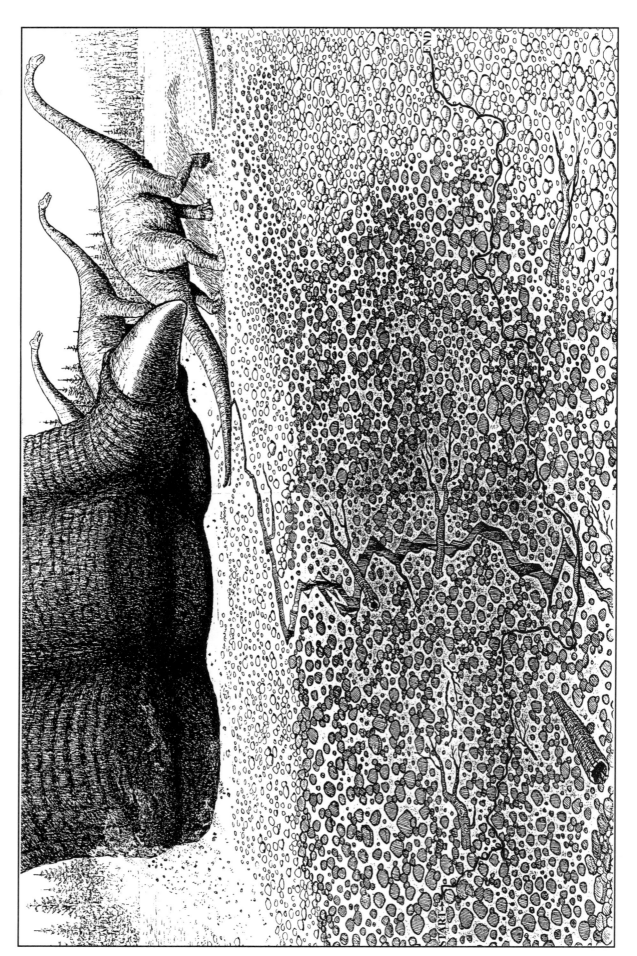

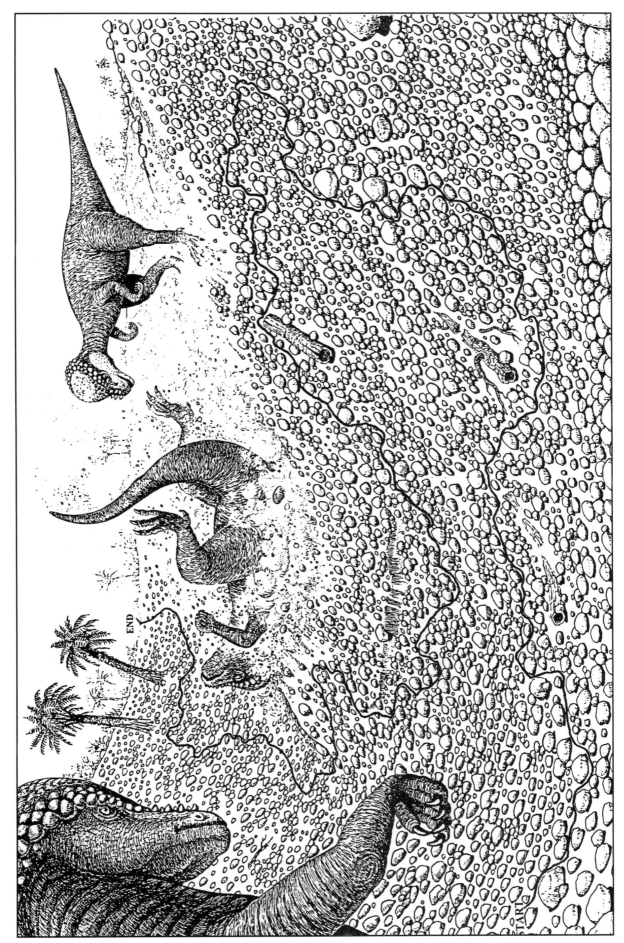

The Tar Pit

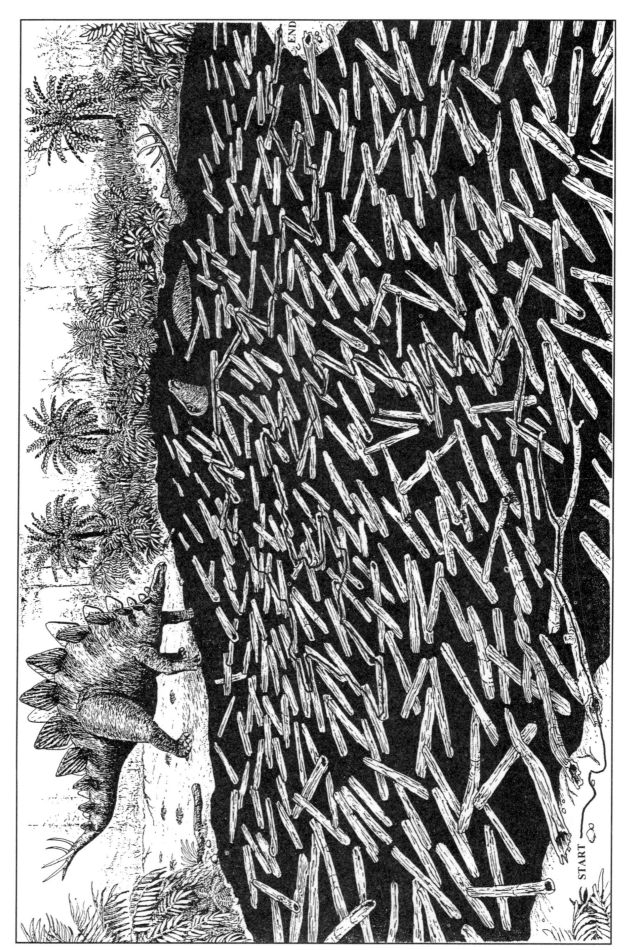

START

END

54

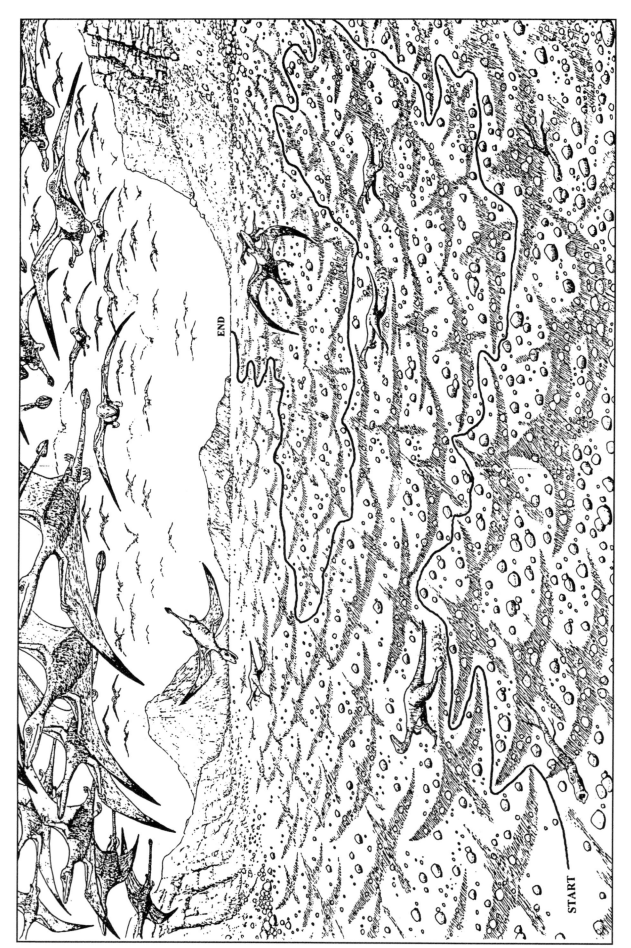

START

END

START

END

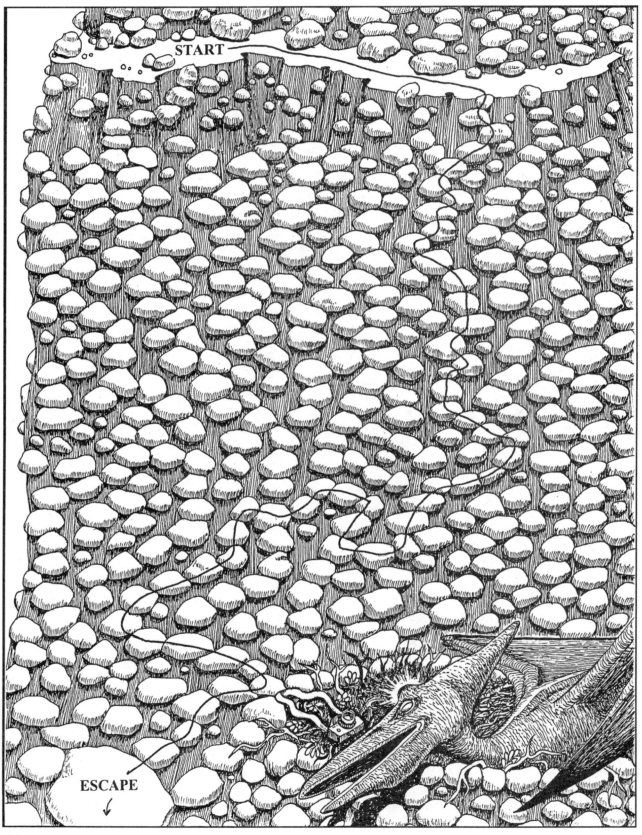

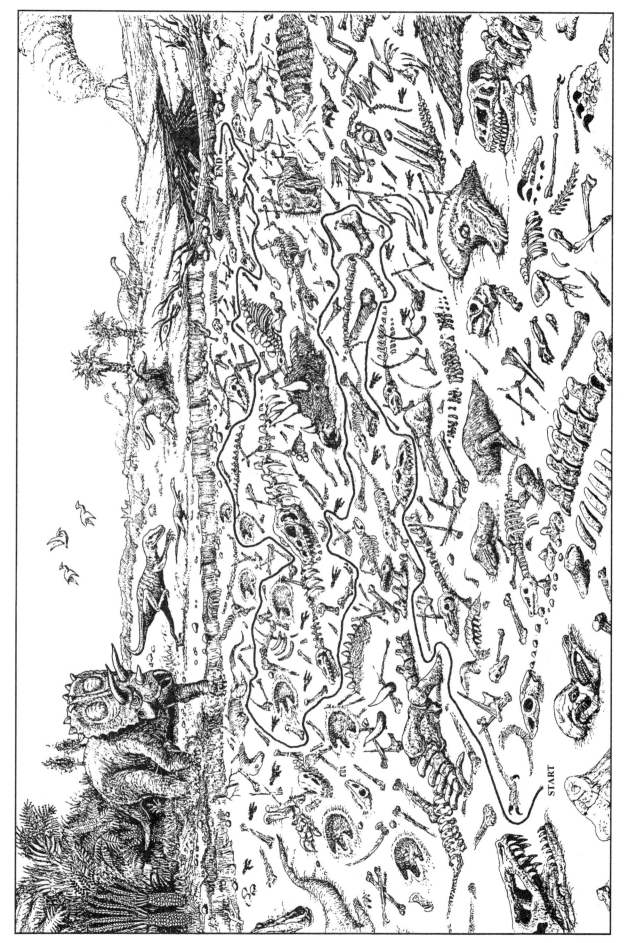

START

END

59

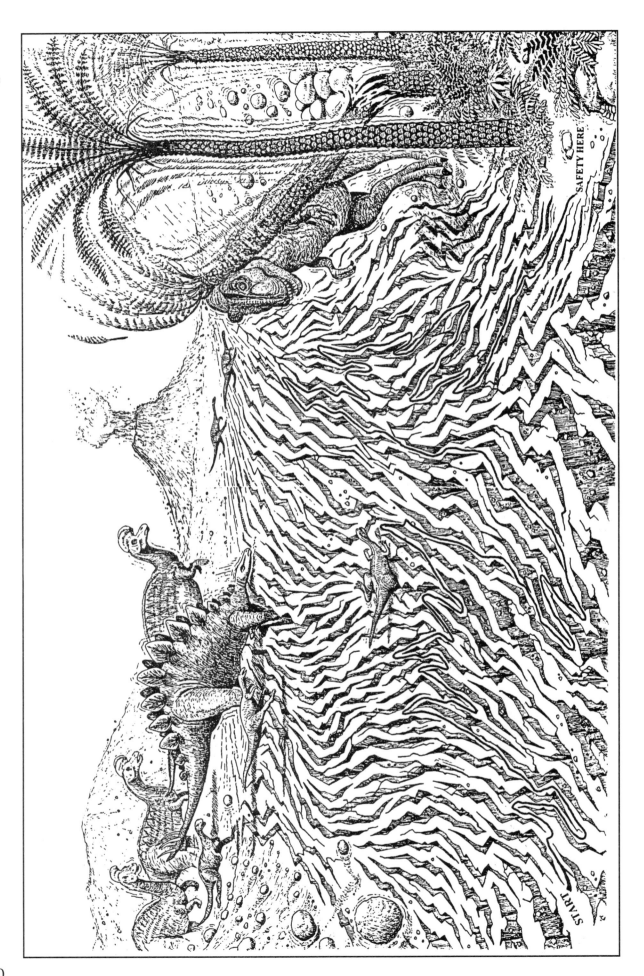

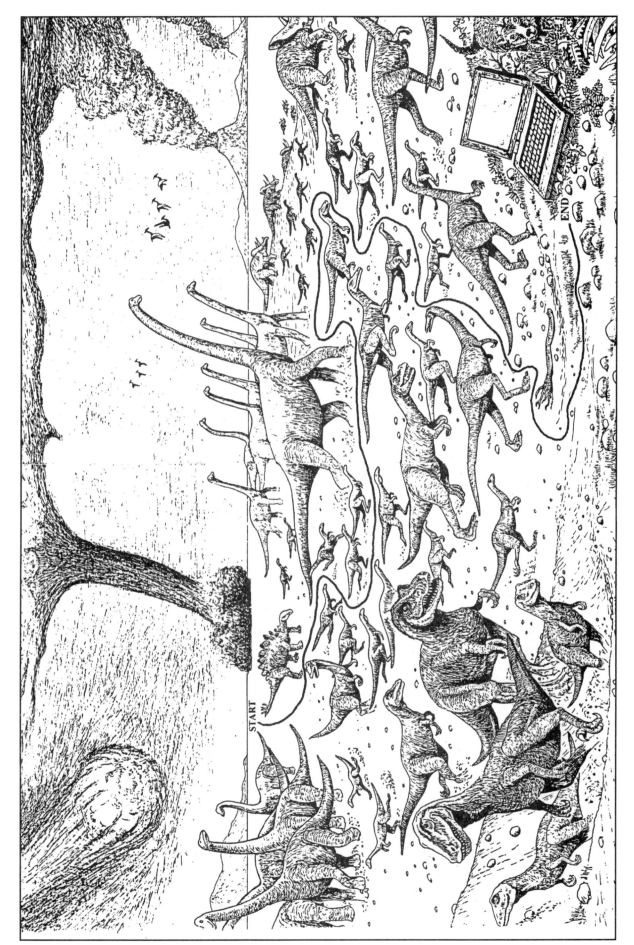

Name the Dinosaurs

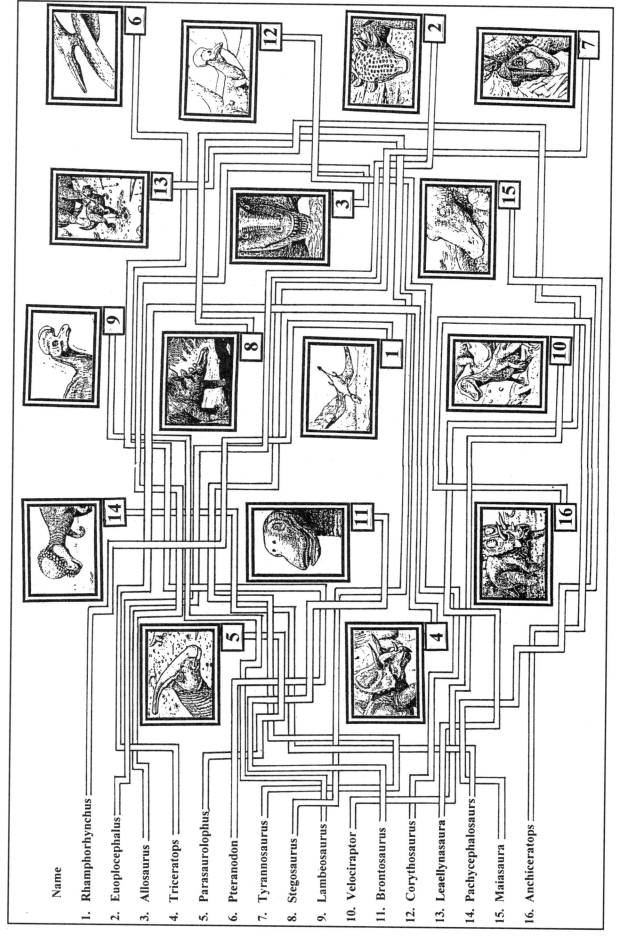

Name

1. Rhamphorhynchus
2. Euoplocephalus
3. Allosaurus
4. Triceratops
5. Parasaurolophus
6. Pteranodon
7. Tyrannosaurus
8. Stegosaurus
9. Lambeosaurus
10. Velociraptor
11. Brontosaurus
12. Corythosaurus
13. Leaellynasaura
14. Pachycephalosaurs
15. Maiasaura
16. Anchiceratops

Index

Numbers in bold refer to mazes, in italics to solutions.